This Is My Life:
A Guided Journal

D1409834

This Is My Life

A Guided Journal

Creative Prompts to Tell Your Story, *So Far*

KRISTEN FOGLE

ROCKRIDGE PRESS

Copyright © 2021 by Rockridge Press, Emeryville, California

No part of this publication may be reproduced, stored in a retrieval system, or transmitted in any form or by any means, electronic, mechanical, photocopying, recording, scanning, or otherwise, except as permitted under Sections 107 or 108 of the 1976 United States Copyright Act, without the prior written permission of the Publisher. Requests to the Publisher for permission should be addressed to the Permissions Department, Rockridge Press, 6005 Shellmound Street, Suite 175, Emeryville, CA 94608.

Limit of Liability/Disclaimer of Warranty: The Publisher and the author make no representations or warranties with respect to the accuracy or completeness of the contents of this work and specifically disclaim all warranties, including without limitation warranties of fitness for a particular purpose. No warranty may be created or extended by sales or promotional materials. The advice and strategies contained herein may not be suitable for every situation. This work is sold with the understanding that the Publisher is not engaged in rendering medical, legal, or other professional advice or services. If professional assistance is required, the services of a competent professional person should be sought. Neither the Publisher nor the author shall be liable for damages arising herefrom. The fact that an individual, organization, or website is referred to in this work as a citation and/or potential source of further information does not mean that the author or the Publisher endorses the information the individual, organization, or website may provide or recommendations they/it may make. Further, readers should be aware that websites listed in this work may have changed or disappeared between when this work was written and when it is read.

For Joey and Declan,
the best part of my story.

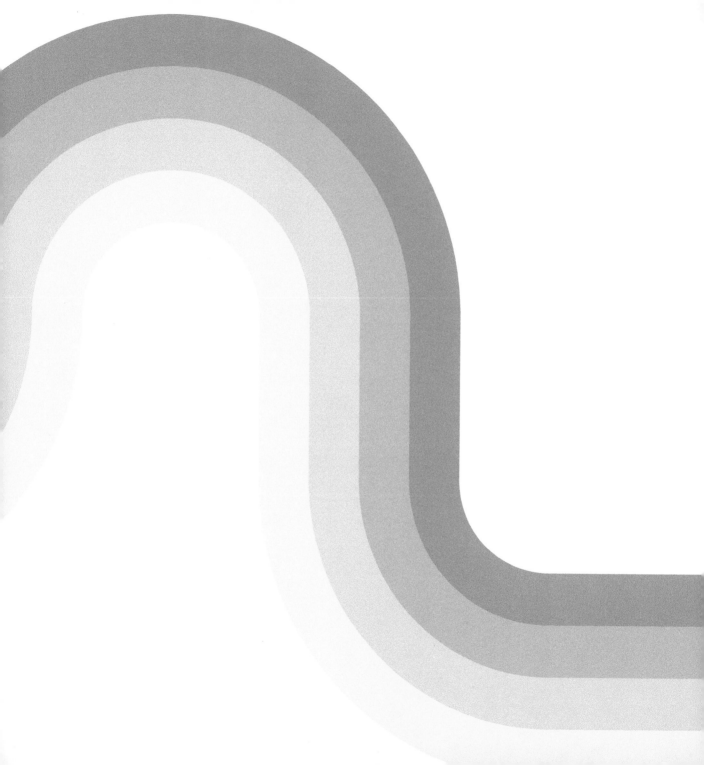

CONTENTS

INTRODUCTION VIII

HOW TO USE THIS BOOK IX

1 **Childhood** 1

2 **Family and Friends** 23

3 **Passions and Pastimes** 47

4 **Work and Career** 67

5 **Community** 85

6 **The Future Me** 107

INTRODUCTION

Hi. I'm Kristen. I'm a writer.

But I wasn't always. I started like most people, writing awkward journal entries and graduating into embarrassing stories about my classmates. In high school I wrote a terrible Dr. Love column, and right after I graduated college I started working at a magazine. That's where I really got hooked on writing. I wrote articles, became an editor, and now I run one of Southern California's largest writing centers. It's a place where people can show up and put words on the page or learn more about a specific style or aspect of writing.

In the almost two decades that I've been writing professionally, however, journaling is still one of my favorite forms. Writing can be hard; getting stuck is real. But when you write about a topic that you know, like yourself, it becomes a little easier. And not only that, but you also get to explore your vast history and uncover things you haven't remembered in years. You can put thoughts into words, often for the first time, and figure out how much (or how little) people, places, and events really meant to you. Sometimes, you even get to reframe the not-so-fun stuff and shape these situations a little differently.

I'm so looking forward to you dipping into your past, present, and future throughout these pages. I hope what you find is magical and delicious. I hope the contents make you reflect, inspire a chuckle, and maybe even make you hopeful for what comes next.

Above all, I hope you fall in love with writing and realize it's not only a tool to explore yourself but also a way to unleash your creativity. As a mentor of mine says, a writer is someone who writes. So welcome to the world of writing. We need more writers like you.

HOW TO USE THIS BOOK

You're ready to go—great! But before you take off down memory lane, let me introduce you to a few things you'll see and explain how you might use this book.

This Is My Life: A Guided Journal is full of ways to express yourself. You might find yourself filling out lists on one page and making a collage or drawing a picture on the next. You'll also find a ton of prompts, and lots and lots of space to get your words down. Follow whatever prompts appeal to you in whatever order you'd like. You can always come back to something later. Whether you dive deep or skim the surface, remember that these prompts are designed to elicit the most interesting and memorable thoughts, feelings, and facts about your life. I've shaped the journal so that you can tackle your life not exactly chronologically, but by topic. Here is a little bit about what you'll find.

» **Chapter 1:** Childhood—This looks at everything from your favorite toys and games to meaningful events and places.

» **Chapter 2:** Family and Friends—Here you can reflect on the people who mean the most, including parents, partners, and even pets.

» **Chapter 3:** Passions and Pastimes—This is where you can share the hobbies, interests, and pleasures that light you up, and why they do.

» **Chapter 4:** Work and Career—Here you can delve into your professional life, including who you met, what you learned, what you accomplished, and more.

» **Chapter 5:** Community—This chapter covers clubs, groups, and other associations that have provided you with a sense of connection.

» **Chapter 6:** The Future Me—To wrap up, you can look ahead to where you'll be years from now, and what you might see when you look back.

Use this book as you wish. It's a great place to dump your thoughts but also an ideal way to start a memoir. You might also make this book a treasured hand-me-down, to show your relatives and future generations all the exciting things that make you you.

ABOUT ME

Let's start by taking a quick inventory of where you are now in life.

DATE

....

MY NAME

....

AGE

....

WHERE I LIVE

....

WHO I LIVE WITH

....

WORK LIFE

....

BEST THING ABOUT LIFE RIGHT NOW

....

WHAT I THINK I'LL USE THIS BOOK FOR

....

1
Childhood

Whether it was smooth sailing or a tad bit rocky at times, the adventure of childhood is one worth recalling. This chapter is the place where you'll unpack that particular box and revisit it all. You'll lay out the mementos, the photos, the lessons, the teachers—the memories that make you unique. And don't worry; whether you were a kiddo just yesterday or decades in the past, there's no wrong way to answer.

IN THE BEGINNING

DATE OF BIRTH

....

WHERE I WAS BORN

....

WHAT MY NAME MEANS AND WHY IT WAS CHOSEN

....

MY EARLIEST NICKNAME

....

MY FIRST CHILDHOOD HOME WAS IN

....

WHEN I WAS BORN, THE U.S. PRESIDENT WAS

....

BIG WORLD EVENTS OF MY CHILDHOOD

....

LATEST TECHNOLOGICAL ADVANCEMENTS OF THAT TIME

....

FAMOUS CELEBRITIES OF THAT TIME

....

MOST POPULAR TV SHOW OF THAT ERA

....

Sometimes your earliest memories really stick. They can be interesting . . . or completely mundane. Record yours here. Where were you and who were you with? What feelings do these memories evoke?

_____

_____

_____

_____

_____

_____

Describe your childhood street. What did the houses or apartments look like? What kinds of birds, trees, and animals did you see? What were the sounds you often heard?

_____

_____

_____

_____

_____

_____

Recall a conversation from when you were a kid. Now put a spin on it and write the scene from a different point of view. (For example, let's take a time when you were punished. How would your parent tell the tale?)

....

....

....

....

....

....

Think about what personality traits you had as a child. Think about your current personality traits. Are you similar or completely different now?

....

....

....

....

....

....

Write about a time when someone cheered you on.

....

....

....

....

....

....

....

Close your eyes. Where was eight-year-old you's favorite place in the world? Somewhere you'd been (or hoped to see) or somewhere completely imagined? Use your five senses and detail it all.?

....

....

....

....

....

....

Did your family celebrate holidays? What traditions or decorations do you recall?

Often what you fought about (or fought for) can show you what you valued when you were young. Pick a fight from your past. Who was it with and what was it about? Does it still matter?

MY CHILDHOOD FAVORITES

BOOK

....

FOOD

....

SONG

....

GAME OR TOY

....

TV SHOW

....

MOVIE

....

CARTOON CHARACTER

....

ACTIVITY

....

PET

....

SPORT

....

PERSON

....

What did you want to be when you were little? What would little you think of what you do now?

....

....

....

....

....

....

Did you have a favorite subject in school? A favorite teacher? What made them stand apart from the others?

....

....

....

....

....

....

....

Time for the opposite. Write about your most disliked subject and teacher here.

....

....

....

....

....

....

Loud music, awkward encounters, corsages, and gowns—school dances could be scary or fun or funny or amazing. Write about your favorite school dance— or reframe a bad one in a new light.

....

....

....

....

....

....

....

Money wasn't always easy to come by for some of us, but we all wanted something. What was something you saved up for? Or something you tried to save up for but didn't get?

_____

_____

_____

_____

_____

_____

When was the first time your parents or guardians gave you a dose of freedom?

_____

_____

_____

_____

_____

_____

_____

Write about an award you received. What was it for? Did you appreciate it then? Describe the ceremony.

....

....

....

....

....

....

Where did your family vacation? Desert, beach, mountains? If there's a place you remember well, record the details here.

....

....

....

....

....

....

....

THE FUN STUFF

On this page, make a fun-time timeline. Chronologically list all the fun things you were into: drawing, skateboarding, surfing, ballet, or whatever else. Circle the hobbies you still participate in.

Besides being incredibly fun at times, special occasions can help shape who you are. Describe one big event and how it influenced your life.

....

....

....

....

....

....

Write about a risk you took when you were young and what the outcome was.

....

....

....

....

....

....

....

Revisit a dream that was either recurring or one that you vividly remember.

_____

_____

_____

_____

_____

_____

Big or small, we were all scared of something. Spiders, clowns, heights—what did you fear growing up?

_____

_____

_____

_____

_____

_____

_____

Were you fashionable? What did you wear? What did you want to wear?

....

....

....

....

....

....

Everyone knew them—kids who made your life miserable. Let's talk about bullies. Who was yours and what were they like? What was their backstory—did they have a reason to be so unpleasant?

....

....

....

....

....

....

....

If you could change one thing about childhood, what would it be?

Celebrities, siblings, cartoons—we all have heroes. Who were yours and what made them so admirable?

RUN WILD: A CHILDHOOD SKETCH

Now fetch some colored pencils or pens. Sketch any of the memories, people, or places you loved revisiting. It could be your childhood home, your pets, a go-to vacation spot, or something else altogether. Really home in on the details, and have fun doing it.

2
Family and Friends

While success is sometimes defined in dollar terms, it is the moments of connection and enjoyment shared with friends, family, and loved ones that bring us the most happiness throughout our lives. At times treasured bonds are forged instantly over an unplanned event. Other times they develop gradually through years of shared experiences—both good and bad.

No matter who have been the most significant people in your life, this is the place to put your memories on the page. From Mom's Monday night poker games, to that date with your first crush, to talking over a plate of your cousin's famous tacos, you have space here to write it all down.

Of course, not every family looks the same, so if you had guardians besides your parents, feel free to write about them instead. The same goes for anyone mentioned in the following pages. Go ahead and trade people out as appropriate. (After all, maybe it's your best friend who made the famous tacos.)

As always, sit back, get comfortable, and relish what comes next.

FAMILY TREE

NAME:

DATE OF BIRTH:

NAME:

DATE OF BIRTH:

NAME:

DATE OF BIRTH:

NAME:

DATE OF BIRTH:

NAME:

DATE OF BIRTH:

NAME:

DATE OF BIRTH:

NAME:

DATE OF BIRTH:

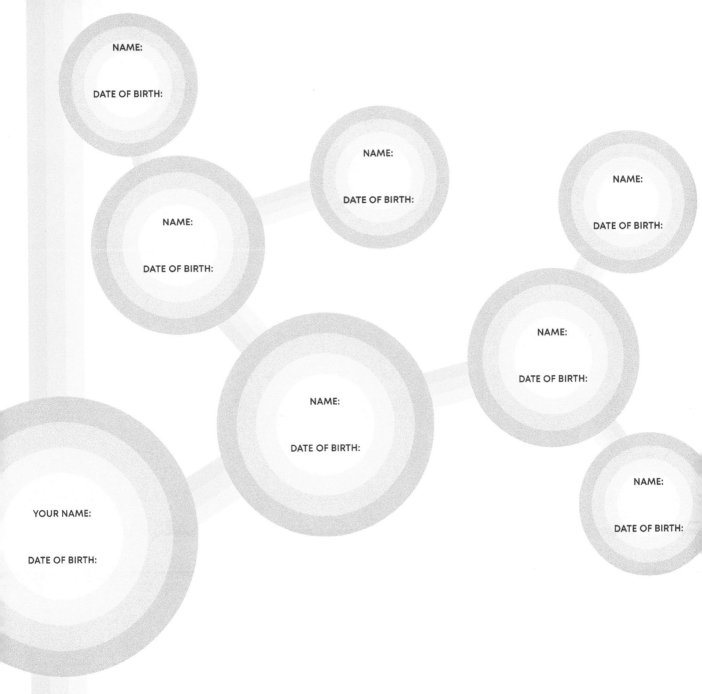

NAME:

DATE OF BIRTH:

NAME:

DATE OF BIRTH:

NAME:

DATE OF BIRTH:

NAME:

DATE OF BIRTH:

NAME:

DATE OF BIRTH:

NAME:

DATE OF BIRTH:

NAME:

DATE OF BIRTH:

YOUR NAME:

DATE OF BIRTH:

Where is your family from? Can you trace their origins?

_____

_____

_____

_____

_____

_____

Describe how your parents met or the story of how another caregiver came into your life.

_____

_____

_____

_____

_____

_____

_____

Describe your mom in three adjectives. Then take one of the adjectives and write down a memory that illustrates that side of her.

....

....

....

....

....

....

What was your relationship with your mom like? How did it change over time?

....

....

....

....

....

....

....

....

....

Now describe your dad in three adjectives. Select one of the adjectives and write down a memory that illustrates it.

....

....

....

....

....

....

What was your relationship with your dad like? How did it change over time?

....

....

....

....

....

....

....

....

Whether by blood, marriage, or choice, who makes up your family today?

....

....

....

....

....

....

If you have children, write down their names and what you value most about them. If you don't have children, write about nephews, nieces, or other children who have been special in your life.

....

....

....

....

....

....

....

....

HOW THINGS TURNED OUT

Write a letter to a teacher, a mentor, or somebody else who made an impression on you in your youth, but who you haven't seen since. What would you tell them about your life? In what ways have you fulfilled or maybe even risen above their expectations for you?

Dear ....

....

....

....

....

....

....

....

....

....

....

....

....

....

Who in your family was the best storyteller? Put their most fabulous yarn on the page.

....

....

....

....

....

Often jewelry, watches, or other heirlooms are handed down in a family or given on special occasions. What artifact bonds you to your family?

....

....

....

....

....

....

....

Did your parents ever take you to work with them? What was that like?

....

....

....

....

....

....

Who was (or is) your favorite extended family member? Describe them in detail.

....

....

....

....

....

....

....

....

....

....

....

Whether it was from a cousin, aunt, grandfather, or someone else, what is something important that a member of your family once said to you?

....

....

....

....

....

....

If you have siblings, write about a time you came together to support each other or accomplish something. If you were an only child, what did you love and dislike about growing up without siblings?

....

....

....

....

....

....

Of all the people you have lived around, who stands out the most? Write about an event in which this person played a major role.

....

....

....

....

....

....

Sometimes a pet is one of our most important loved ones. List everything you loved about your first or your favorite pet.

....

....

....

....

....

....

....

Was there a spiritual leader or an influential thinker you looked up to?
Was there something they said that sticks in your mind?

....

....

....

....

....

....

School is full of cliques. Close your eyes and imagine the place where your group hung out—describe it using your five senses. Think about something significant that happened there and write about that, too.

....

....

....

....

....

....

How would you describe each of your siblings? If you are an only child, write about someone who took on a sibling-like role in your life.

....

....

....

....

....

....

What do you hope your children or the young people in your life have learned from you? Conversely, what have they taught you?

....

....

....

....

....

....

....

A LITTLE HELP FROM MY FRIENDS

While acquaintances come and go, our true friends have such an impact on who we become. Think about each of these types of friends below. After you've identified them, try to recall and record a vivid memory about each one.

THE MOST LOYAL FRIEND

....

THE FRIEND WHO WAS THE MOST FUN

....

THE FRIEND WHO PUSHED YOU TO DO BETTER

....

THE FRIEND WHO YOU GREW APART FROM

....

THE FRIEND WHO WAS YOUR CONFIDANT

....

THE FRIEND WHO WAS COMPLETELY DIFFERENT FROM YOU

....

THE FRIEND WHO GOT YOU IN TROUBLE

....

Who was your first crush and when did you know you had a crush on them? Did they ever find out?

....

....

....

....

....

....

Write about a date that went badly with someone who you really love (or loved).

....

....

....

....

....

....

....

Choose a date that was really special. Try to tell it from the perspective of an impartial observer, so you can look in on that occasion in a slightly different way.

....

....

....

....

....

....

How did you meet the love of your life? If you haven't met the love of your life yet, describe them as if you already have.

....

....

....

....

....

....

A wedding can be among the most memorable days of our lives. If you had one, describe the day. If you never had one (or would rather forget it), write about a special celebration with a loved one.

....

....

....

....

....

....

What is the secret to a long-lasting romance?

....

....

....

....

....

....

....

RUN WILD: A COLLAGE FOR LOVED ONES

Get out some images—photos, magazines, or anything else—some scissors, and your trusty glue stick. It's time for you to choose a person or people you wrote about in this chapter and assemble a collage of creative images and fun items that remind you of them. Feel free to draw your own sketches, too.

Notes about the collage:

....

....

3
Passions and Pastimes

While your passions and pastimes may sometimes seem like footnotes in the story of your life, in reality they reveal a great deal about what makes you tick, what brings you joy, and who you really are outside of your professional life. After all, it is through your hobbies, interests, and leisure time that you are often at your most curious, creative, and content.

In this chapter you will do a deep dive into all the things that light you up. You will reminisce about things you collect, trips you have taken, games you like to play, and plenty more. You will cover the highbrow, the lowbrow, and the in-between. Be honest, get into it, and as always, enjoy.

THE SOUNDTRACK OF MY LIFE

Songs have a special way of transporting us to a particular time and place. On the next few pages, you can piece together a soundtrack to your life with the songs that have defined it and the memories or feelings they bring up.

	SONG AND ARTIST	MEMORY OR FEELING
THE SONG THAT SUMS UP MY PERSONALITY		
THE SONG THAT REMINDS ME OF HIGH SCHOOL		
MY FAVORITE LOVE SONG		
THE SONG THAT CAN MAKE ME CRY		

	SONG AND ARTIST	MEMORY OR FEELING
MY KARAOKE ANTHEM		
THE SONG THAT ALWAYS GETS ME DANCING		
THE SONG THAT GOT ME THROUGH HARD TIMES		
THE SONG I WANT PLAYED AT MY FUNERAL		

Did you belong to any clubs in or out of school? Which ones?

Stamps, clocks, trains—lots of people collect things. Over your lifetime, have you had any collections? What were they?

Who has most encouraged your interests in life? How has their support helped you grow?

_____

_____

_____

_____

_____

_____

Many people have skills beyond their jobs. What are some of yours? Think of a time when you surprised someone with your expertise.

_____

_____

_____

_____

_____

_____

Have you ever been a teacher of some sort? What was most rewarding about that experience? If you have never taught, what do you think you would be good at teaching?

....

....

....

....

....

....

When people ask you what you do for fun, what do you tell them? Is there anything you leave out?

....

....

....

....

....

....

....

FINDING MY BLISS

THE WAY I RECHARGE IS

....

MY TOP THREE SIMPLE PLEASURES IN LIFE ARE

....

MY MOTTO FOR ENJOYING LIFE IS

....

MY IDEAL DAY WOULD BE

....

TRUE HAPPINESS IS

....

HARMONY IN THE WORLD LOOKS LIKE

....

Dribbling, diving, passing, putting—what sports do you love to watch?

Which ones do you love to play?

....

....

....

....

....

....

What's one gift you received that sparked a future interest?

....

....

....

....

....

....

....

....

We all have them—people who leave us absolutely starstruck. Name any celebrities you've met in person. Any good (or bad) stories about them are appropriate here!

....

....

....

....

....

....

What are some TV shows you could watch over and over? What do you love most about them?

....

....

....

....

....

....

What are your favorite book genres? What kinds of stories pull you in? Has this changed over time?

....

....

....

....

....

....

Food is a delicious interest all on its own. Describe one of the most memorable meals you have ever cooked or eaten.

....

....

....

....

....

....

....

....

What was the first concert you went to? What was your favorite concert ever?

_____

_____

_____

_____

_____

What languages do you know how to speak? What languages do you wish you knew?

_____

_____

_____

_____

_____

_____

_____

Van Gogh or Banksy? Modernism or impressionism? Who are your favorite artists? Would you consider yourself artistic?

....

....

....

....

....

....

Have you ever made a piece of art or undertaken another creative venture like music, acting, or something else altogether? What did you make or perform?

....

....

....

....

....

....

....

MY BUCKET LIST

Whether it's skydiving or seeing the Great Pyramid of Giza, write down the things that you have—and haven't yet—ticked off your bucket list.

THINGS I'VE TICKED OFF MY BUCKET LIST

1. ....

2. ....

3. ....

4. ....

5. ....

THINGS STILL ON MY BUCKET LIST

1. ....

2. ....

3. ....

4. ....

5. ....

Are you an animal lover? What are some of your favorites?

It is sometimes said that clothes make the person. Do you place value on how you dress? How would you describe your personal style?

Do you love cozying up in indoor spaces or are you more a fan of the great outdoors? Pick a place that speaks to you and write about a good time you had there.

....

....

....

....

....

....

How would you describe your religious, spiritual, or philosophical beliefs? Have they changed over time?

....

....

....

....

....

....

Are you a fan of politics? Why or why not?

....

....

....

....

....

....

....

We all need them—activities that help us wind down. What do you do to relax?

....

....

....

....

....

....

....

RUN WILD: A MEMORABLE TRIP

Whether you've been to Bali or Boston, far from home or just a few blocks away, travels are fun to recall. Think of a trip you really loved. Is there a photo you took then that comes to mind now? Or maybe just a mental picture of the scenery or a person you met there? Whatever is in your head, re-create it below. If you prefer, you can simply paste some of the photos instead.

4
Work and Career

It's been estimated that we spend one-third of our life working. That's a lot! So it's pretty safe to say that you probably have had some fun times on the job (like dancing the night away at that office party) and some not-so-great times (like staying late to finish a project that wasn't really yours to begin with).

Whether you've had dream jobs or they've mostly been drudgery, there's a lot to unpack here. After all, work isn't just about the hours logged. It's about what you accomplished, the lessons you learned, and the people you'll never forget.

Maybe you were a homemaker or a caregiver, or your career was a bit less traditional. That's okay! These jobs are just as important as, if not more important than, the traditional nine to five. Just go ahead and reframe the questions as you see fit. This is all about your life and your particular circumstances.

THE CAREER REVIEW

FIRST JOB

....

MOST RECENT JOB

....

JOB I HAD FOR THE LONGEST TIME

....

JOB I HAD FOR THE SHORTEST TIME

....

JOB WHERE I MADE A GOOD FRIEND

....

MOST LUCRATIVE JOB

....

LEAST LUCRATIVE JOB

....

JOB WITH THE LONGEST COMMUTE

....

JOB WITH THE SHORTEST COMMUTE

....

JOB I WISH I COULD HAVE AGAIN

....

A first job is always memorable. What was yours like?

_____

_____

_____

_____

_____

_____

The interview process can be nerve-wracking or exciting. Do you remember a particularly memorable one? What happened? Did you get the job?

_____

_____

_____

_____

_____

_____

_____

They ask these questions at an interview, so we will ask them here. What do you consider your biggest weakness?

....

....

....

....

....

....

....

What's your biggest strength?

....

....

....

....

....

....

....

Colleges, certificates, training—what education did you receive that was most helpful in your career?

_____

_____

_____

_____

_____

_____

If you had to do it all over again, what kind of education or training would you get?

_____

_____

_____

_____

_____

_____

_____

Who was your best work friend? How did your friendship form?

....

....

....

....

....

....

Who was your least favorite colleague or boss? Do you have an amusing memory about them?

....

....

....

....

....

....

....

....

THE LESSONS I'VE LEARNED

This is the time to catalogue all the things you learned on the job. They can be lofty or little, but they should be meaningful lessons.

THE WORK FAIL THAT TAUGHT ME A LOT

....

THE EMBARRASSING MOMENT ON THE JOB

....

THE PRACTICAL SKILL I GAINED FROM WORK

....

THE PERSON WHO GUIDED ME

....

THE WISDOM I RECEIVED AT WORK

....

Did you ever win awards or receive recognition on the job? Write about those here. Include info about certificates, ceremonies, or times you felt really proud of yourself.

....

....

....

....

....

Write about the job you enjoyed most. What made it so amazing?

....

....

....

....

....

....

....

Write about a job you hated. How long did you stay?

_____

_____

_____

_____

_____

_____

We all have careers we think would be amazing to have. If you could create the perfect job, what would it look like?

_____

_____

_____

_____

_____

_____

_____

_____

Not all jobs last forever. Write about a time when you chose to leave (or a time you were asked to).

....

....

....

....

....

....

Some leaders are inspiring and some aren't. What did a boss teach you by doing it the wrong way?

....

....

....

....

....

....

....

....

What's the longest you went without working? Why?

_____

_____

_____

_____

_____

_____

Have you ever had to wear a uniform to work? If not, was there a time in your life that you wore something fun, silly, or memorable in the workplace? Write a day-in-the-life of that job.

_____

_____

_____

_____

_____

_____

WORDS OF WISDOM

Imagine you are writing a letter to your child, grandchild, or even your younger self with advice about work. What is the value of hard work? What is the best approach to striking a balance between labor and leisure? What do you wish someone had told you when you finished school and ventured out into the world?

Taking care of a home is a job of its own. What are you most proud of having done in your current home or in a previous one?

....

....

....

....

....

....

It is sometimes said that money can't buy happiness. To what extent do you agree or disagree?

....

....

....

....

....

....

....

Think about the job you have now or your previous job. If you had to write three adjectives to describe it, what would they be? Then pick one of those adjectives. What story exemplifies it?

....

....

....

....

....

....

If you have retired, describe how you have made the most of it. If you are still working, what are your goals for retirement?

....

....

....

....

....

....

RUN WILD: WORK MEMENTOS

Do you have any mementos or souvenirs from your jobs? The following space is for all of that—receipts to remember those fancy client dinners, movie stubs from your days as an usher, business cards from previous roles, or maybe a photo of you at work. See what you can find, and glue to your heart's content. Don't have any mementos stored away? Draw what you might have saved.

5
Community

When you look at your whole life, there are so many communities that you have been, and maybe currently are, a part of. These include groups you choose to associate with and belong to—clubs, religious organizations, and the like—and others you are brought closer to by geography or circumstances, such as a community of neighbors.

Both say a lot about where you came from and where you're going. So grab a pen and dig in—let's see what your affiliations uncover.

THE COMMUNITIES THAT SHAPED ME

The communities you are a part of can have a lasting impact on your life. For each of the following prompts, describe each group and how they helped shape who you are today.

MY CHILDHOOD COMMUNITY

....

MY GROUP IN MY TEENAGE YEARS

....

MY SPORTING OR ACTIVITY CLUB

....

MY PROFESSIONAL OR OFFICIAL ORGANIZATION

....

MY CULTURAL COMMUNITY

....

Teams, effective ones anyhow, often share a sense of purpose and like-minded goals. List a team you have been on, the ideal you shared, and what you achieved.

....
....
....
....
....
....

Let's consider classmates. Did you grow up with the same group of people or were they always changing? Who stands out to you? Why?

....
....
....
....
....
....
....

Were the kids in your neighborhood different from those you went to school with? Write about those differences. Or, if it was the same group, how did roles and games change after the bell rang?

....

....

....

....

....

....

Your surroundings can also be part of your community. What type of environment makes you feel one with nature?

....

....

....

....

....

....

Be it a comfy suburban street, a chic condo block in the city, or a place in the country, describe your favorite community of neighbors you have lived among.

What 'urban legends' are there about places in your area or one you have previously lived in?

How much does your neighborhood define who you are?

....

....

....

....

....

....

Maybe it's not your neighborhood but your town, region, state, or country you really identify with. What values would you say align you with this group of people?

....

....

....

....

....

....

Tents, campfires, s'mores—all these call to mind summer camp. Did you ever go to one, or on an outdoor adventure of some sort? Describe how you felt and the people you met.

....

....

....

....

....

....

Were you ever in a sorority or fraternity? Or maybe an after-school or college group? Or perhaps you served in the military? What's the funniest or craziest story you recall from this time?

....

....

....

....

....

....

A COMMON CAUSE

Often the spheres we find ourselves in revolve around the causes we are passionate about. What political, religious, charity, or volunteer group has been especially meaningful in your life? Fill in the details here.

THE GROUP OR COMMUNITY

....

THE VALUES IT REPRESENTS

....

HOW WE HELPED OTHERS

....

HOW I PERSONALLY CONTRIBUTED

....

A HAPPY MEMORY

....

What's a project you worked on in a group (in or out of work) that gave you a sense of pride? What did you accomplish together?

....

....

....

....

....

....

Let's go the opposite way. Whether it was a group you were assigned to during a class, a place you lived where you didn't fit in, or an awkward work assignment, write about a time when you knew the company you kept just weren't your people.

....

....

....

....

....

....

Pick a life event—a celebration or perhaps a tragedy—that bonded you to others you may not have known before then.

....

....

....

....

....

....

Sometimes travel can bring out unexpected aspects of yourself and others. Pick a time when traveling with others brought out the best (or worst) in you.

....

....

....

....

....

....

....

Think about a cultural community you belong or belonged to. What events, festivals, holidays, or activities do you love most about this group?

....

....

....

....

....

....

Spiritual or religious group members can share a bond like no other. Do you have any experiences in these types of groups?

....

....

....

....

....

....

....

Who is a community leader you admire? Why?

_____

_____

_____

_____

_____

_____

What are your thoughts about social media? Have you used it to reconnect with anyone?

_____

_____

_____

_____

_____

_____

THE ROLES WE PLAY

Think of who or what you consider the most important community in your life. Perhaps it is your extended family, the neighborhood you live in, or another group altogether. Who would you nominate to fulfill the following roles?

THE HERO

....

THE CHEERLEADER

....

THE ECCENTRIC

....

THE PERFECTIONIST

....

THE COMEDIAN

....

THE CONFIDANT

....

THE TROUBLEMAKER

....

THE CAREGIVER

....

THE PEACEMAKER

....

FINALLY, DESCRIBE THE ROLE YOU PLAY IN YOUR OWN GROUP OR COMMUNITY.

....

We've talked about family members, but let's look at your family as a unit. What was a moment that made you feel especially bonded to your family as a kid?

....

....

....

....

....

....

....

What about as an adult?

....

....

....

....

....

....

....

What do you need or what might need to happen to further bond you with your family?

....

....

....

....

....

....

Who is your found family, your chosen people whom you are closest to?

....

....

....

....

....

....

....

What do you and most of your long-standing friends have in common?

_____

_____

_____

_____

_____

_____

What's your ideal community now?

_____

_____

_____

_____

_____

_____

RUN WILD: BADGE OF HONOR

Pick one or a few of the communities or causes you wrote about in this chapter. Draw or paste in one or more of their emblems or logos. This could take the form of a national flag, spiritual symbols, coats of arms, a crest, or something else. Can't think of any? Choose one of your groups and create your own emblem or logo.

6

The Future Me

Everything you've written about so far has actually happened. From here on out you'll imagine what hasn't happened yet.

Now is the time to look forward—as many days, weeks, years, or decades as you're comfortable with. You can explore what your life might be like in the future, through the unique perspective of present day. Except for the box Where I See Myself (page 108), there's no set date for this look ahead. Feel free to choose a future date for particular questions if you wish, though.

This is also a section to survey the work you've done so far in this book, which is your invitation to think about everything you've put down and see what matters, and maybe even set some goals. There's a place here for that, too.

WHERE I SEE MYSELF

Answer some quick questions about your future self. First, circle how many years in the future you'd like to go:

1 YEAR   **10 YEARS**

5 YEARS   **20 YEARS**

Take a moment to envision the life you hope to lead in that many years' time. Then fill in the following blanks, answering as your future self.

WHERE I LIVE AND/OR WORK   **THE PERSON I RECONNECTED WITH**

....

....

THE PEOPLE I SEE THE MOST   **A NEW PLACE I HAVE TRAVELED TO**

....

....

A FAMILIAR PLACE I HAVE REVISITED

....

....

SOMETHING I HAVE LEARNED

....

....

A FEAR I HAVE OVERCOME

....

....

WHAT I AM MOST THANKFUL FOR

....

....

THE BIGGEST CHANGE IN MY LIFE

....

....

THE BIGGEST CHANGE IN THE WORLD

....

....

Who are the people who will be most important to you in the years to come?

....

....

....

....

....

....

Close your eyes. What does your ideal future sound like?

....

....

....

....

....

....

....

....

Think more about where you want to live. What does your dream home look like?

....

....

....

....

....

....

What creative projects might you undertake in the future? (You can refer back to your fun-time timeline on page 14 for some ideas.)

....

....

....

....

....

....

....

....

Ideally, how do you spend your days?

....

....

....

....

....

....

Eventually, what do you want to be remembered for?

....

....

....

....

....

....

....

MY WILDEST DREAM

What's your wildest dream for the future? The bigger and more audacious, the better. Now that you have it, how can you make a little—or a lot—of that dream come true?

THE DREAM

....

THE FIRST SMALL STEP

....

THE BIGGEST OBSTACLE

....

THE LARGER STEPS REQUIRED

....

HOW I WILL MEASURE SUCCESS

....

What health changes do you hope to make?

_____

_____

_____

_____

_____

_____

What bad habits do you hope to break?

_____

_____

_____

_____

_____

_____

_____

What good habits do you hope to form?

....

....

....

....

....

....

....

What is the grudge you hope to bury?

....

....

....

....

....

....

....

What do you want your future self to remember most about your life right now?

....

....

....

....

....

....

What do you want your future self to remember most about this time in history?

....

....

....

....

....

....

....

You've explored your wildest dream, so let's look at some other goals. What is the most important thing for you to accomplish in:

THE NEXT MONTH

....

....

....

THE NEXT SIX MONTHS

....

....

....

THE NEXT YEAR

....

....

....

THE NEXT DECADE

....

....

....

Aside from your family members or close friends having material and professional security, what happiness do you hope they attain?

_____

_____

_____

_____

_____

_____

If you could write your own epitaph or memorial plaque, what would you write?

_____

_____

_____

_____

_____

_____

TAKING STOCK

Let's look back at the previous five chapters. Have you been surprised by any recollections? Gained insight into your past or present? Felt proud of particular successes? What are your biggest takeaways from each?

CHILDHOOD

....

FAMILY AND FRIENDS

....

PASSIONS AND PASTIMES

....

WORK AND CAREER

....

COMMUNITY

....

If your life was turned into a Hollywood biopic, which actor would you like to play you?

_____

_____

_____

_____

_____

_____

What medical and technological advances would you like to see? How might they change the world?

_____

_____

_____

_____

_____

_____

_____

What stories, events, or people haven't you explored yet in this book that your future self might want to remember?

....

....

....

....

....

....

Thinking of the lessons you have learned in life, what is the best piece of advice you would give to your grandchildren or young people in general?

....

....

....

....

....

....

....

....

Finally, write down the things that make you feel optimistic about the future.

RUN WILD: VISION BOARD

Thinking creatively or visually about your future can spark interesting thoughts or help clarify your hopes, wishes, and priorities. Use this page to create a vision board for your future. This could include a collage of images, inspiring quotes or mantras, and even sketches of what you hope for. Think of the key areas of your life—relationships, family, health, home, and personal growth—and let your creativity run wild.

ABOUT THE AUTHOR

Kristen Fogle has been the executive director of San Diego Writers, Ink, a nonprofit literary center, since 2013. She is also a writing instructor, teaching artist, and theatrical producer, director, and performer. Her first book, *Dare to Write*, was published by Rockridge Press in 2019. Find out more at KristenFogle.com or SanDiegoWriters.org.